Anna Bjärkvik

A visionary woman, yogi, fashion designer, author and mother who wish for children and adults alike to connect to their inner spark of magic!

Caroline Midbeck

A Swedish artist who makes magic and wonder come alive through her works. As a mother and art teacher, she is also passionate about raising the creativity within others.

© Text: Anna Bjärkvik
© Illustrations: Caroline Midbeck
Soul talk AB, Glemmingebro 2020
Cover and design: Johan Silver
English translation: Laura Geiger
Author photo: Anna Hållams

ISBN: 978-91-986226-0-7

www.annabjarkvik.com

A Feeling of Me

ANNA BJÄRKVIK
CAROLINE MIDBECK

ENGLISH TRANSLATION LAURA GEIGER

Hello!

I'm glad that you are here.

It's going to be so fun to follow along as you find
out how it feels to be you.

Are you ready?

Have you ever felt your feet?

Feel how soft they are and how nice it is to
touch them.

Are the bottoms of your feet ticklish?

Think how wonderful your little feet are!
They help you run and dance and jump and
walk around to discover the world.

Can you count your toes?

Did you know that love brought you to the earth?
It was the love between your parents. And the Universe's
love for children, of course.

What a terrific feeling it is to love someone. We want that
person to be near, and our hearts hurt a little when they
are gone too long. But in your own heart, love is always
nearby.

Can you feel your heart beating and thumping inside your
chest? Listen to someone else's heart. It is full of love, too.

You might know people who can be really
grumpy or angry.

You know what? Their hearts are full of the
same amount of love as yours. It's just that life
has given them a sort of shield around their
hearts to help them hurt less.

A shield makes it hard for love to reach out.

Do you sometimes hide behind an invisible
shield when life feels hard?

Ever since you came out of your mommy's belly, you have
been breathing. Can you feel your breath?

Feel how it slides through your throat like an air elevator:

down and up
down and up
down and up

Cover your ears and breathe. How does it sound?
Like the sea?
Like someone who is sound asleep?
Like whistling in the trees?

Your spine is so cool. It's like a long snake that
can bend and twist and zigzag.

Try to bend backwards like a cobra. *Ssss*
Round your back like a cat. *Meow*
Let your belly sag toward the floor and
stretch your neck up like a cow. *Moo*

Swing and sway your spine to make a cool
little dance.

Whew! How does your back feel now? Does it
feel warm anywhere? Does your body tingle?

Ssssssss...
MUUUuuuu
MIAU miau
...

Do you know where your pelvis is?

It's a nice, safe spot in everyone's body, a little like a magic cave.

It was in your mommy's pelvis that you were made. You grew and grew, and your mommy's belly became big and round. It got so crowded that you wanted out!

Do you remember how it felt in there?

You could say that the Universe made a very special
work of art inside your mommy's belly, one that came
to make the world a little more beautiful in its own
special way.

That artwork is you!
The next time you see your reflection in the mirror, look
carefully at what a perfect person the Universe made.

She did her very, very best work.

JAG

Do you sometimes sit on the ground?

Trees and flowers are connected to the earth.
Can you sit on the ground and feel that you are
connected, too?

You can pretend that you are a tree with roots deep
in the earth beneath you. Even in stormy winds,
you feel strong and steady.

Hands are amazing tools that can do so many
things. They are good for eating, clapping, touching
someone's cheek, building a fort, or throwing a ball.

What else can you think of?

Can you use your hands like feet?

Rub your hands together fast until they get warm
and tingly. Cover your eyes with your warm hands.
Do you see only darkness, or is something else there?

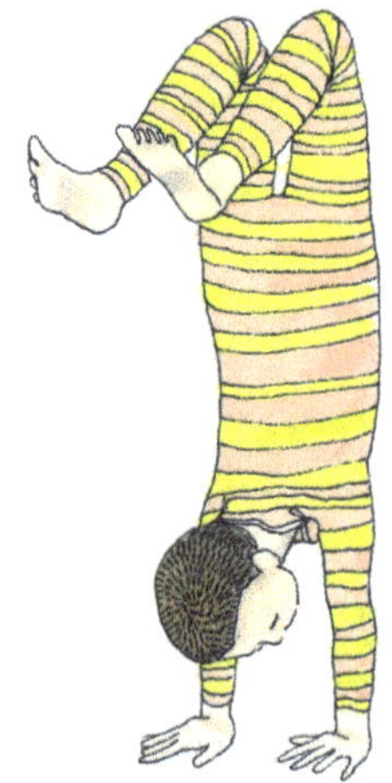

1
2
3
6
17
8
5
9
10

Feelings are kind of like clouds in the sky. They
move around all the time, and you can't really
control them.

Sometimes feeling-clouds are big and grumpy.
Other times, there are no clouds at all, only
sunshine and happiness.

How does it feel inside you right now?

Pat your belly until it feels cheerful and content.

Put your hands over your heart and feel how your heart is smiling in there.

Smile with your face and send the smile all the way down to your toes.

You can feel really proud and happy that you are you!